Jellyfish

Robbie Byerly

This is jelly.

This is a fish.

This is a jellyfish.

Jellyfish live in the water.

They look like where they live.

Jellyfish look like the rocks.

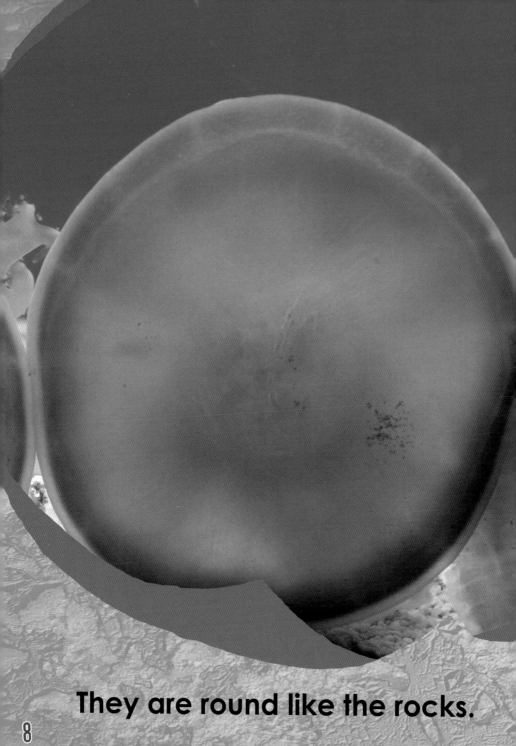

They are round like the rocks.

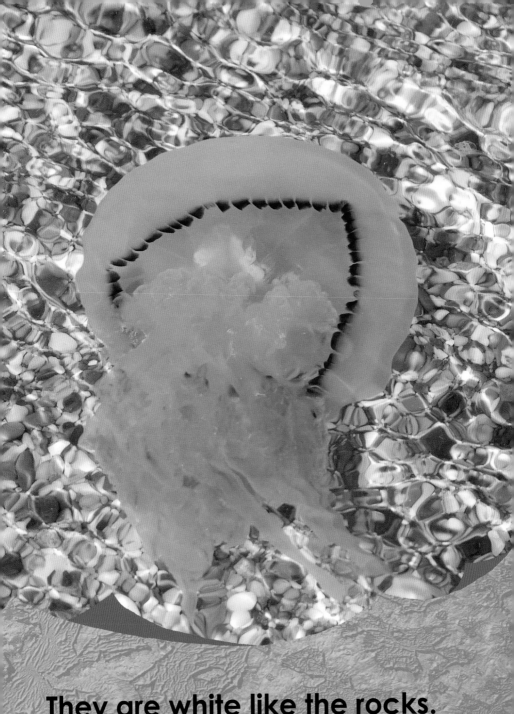

They are white like the rocks.

This is a plant.

There are plants in the water.

Jellyfish look like the plants.

Why do jellyfish look like where they live?

These are little fish.

Little fish live in the plants.

The little fish can't see the
jellyfish in the plants.

Jellyfish eat the little fish.

Sea turtles eat jellyfish.

When the jellyfish are in the rocks, the sea turtle can't get them.

Octopuses eat jellyfish.

When the jellyfish are in the plants,
the octopuses can't see them.

This is why jellyfish look
like where they live.

Word Attack Strategies
Tips for Tricky Words

STOP	**Stop** if something doesn't look right, sound right, or make sense.
	Think about what's happening in the story/text.
	Look at the **picture**.
t___	Say the **first letter** sound.
th___	**Blend:** Say the first two letters.
←	**Reread:** Go back and try again.
blank	Say "**blank**," read on, and come back.

Power

a	eat	like
are	get	little
can't	in	live
do	is	look